DO AS I SAY

Operations, Procedures, and Rituals
for
Language Acquisition

Gayle Nelson, Thomas Winters, Raymond C. Clark

with illustrations by T.D. Whistler and A. Mario Fantini

PRO LINGUA  **ASSOCIATES**

Pro Lingua Associates, Publishers
P.O. Box 1348
Brattleboro, Vermont 05302 USA
Office: 802 257 7779
Orders: 800 366 4775
E-mail: info@ProLinguaAssociates.com
WebStore: www.ProLinguaAssociates.com
SAN: 216-0579

At Pro Lingua
our objective is to foster an approach
to learning and teaching that we call
Interplay, the **inter**action of language
learners and teachers with their materials,
with the language and culture,
and with each other in active, creative
and productive **play**.

ISBN 0-86647-159-6: 978-0-86647-159-6

Many of the illustrations are by T.D. Whistler and A. Mario Fantini. Others were selected from two clip art collections: Art Explosion®: 750,000 Images, Copyright ©1995-2000 by Nova Development Corporation and its licensors; The Big Box of Art™, Copyright ©1997-2002 by Hermera Technologies Inc. and its licensors.

This book was designed by Arthur A. Burrows and set by him in Trebuchet MS, a slightly whimsical sanserif font, and using as a display type a font called Comic Sans MS, a bolder, more caligraphic sanserif intended to suggest the script used in comic books; both fonts from Adobe. It was printed and bound by McNaughton & Gunn in Saline, Michigan.

Third, revised edition, second revised printing 2007
7,000 copies of the Pro Lingua editions in print.
Printed in the United States of America

Publishers' Foreword

Do As I Say was originally published in 1980 by Newbury House as *ESL Operations* by Gayle Nelson and Thomas Winters. In 1993 Pro Lingua republished the book in a new, revised edition as *Operations in English,* and reprinted it in 2002. Although much of the original material has been retained in this edition, we have made many changes, as indicated by the new title and sub-title, *Do As I Say: Operations, Procedures, and Rituals for Language Acquisition.*

The original Newbury House edition contained 41 "operations." In the 1993 edition, there were 55 "operations." In this edition, a few have been deleted, many have been modified, and there are now 75 "sequences." In other words there have been many changes since the original 1980 edition.

We are now pleased to offer this new edition as a photocopyable book in a more convenient 8 1/2 x 11 format.

We would like to express our thanks to Gayle and Tom for giving us permission to update, revise, and change their original text.

Authors' Acknowledgements

We wish to express our thanks to the students and staff of the School for International Training for their suggestions and support as we developed the original edition. We thank Mary Clark and Pat Byrd for helping us with grammar notes. And special thanks to Ray Clark for initiating the original project and continuing to work with us as editor and as a co-author of this new edition.

We also had contributions from a number of graduate students at Georgia State University. Specifically, we would like to thank Ron Summer for "Using a Calculator," Harold Rowland for "Making an Origami Cicada," Lauren Gold for "Making Popcorn," and Tony Dickenson for "Using a Fast Food Drive-Through."

Gayle Nelson
Thomas Winters

Contents

Contents

Household Activities

Games and Exercises

Contents

Food and Recipes

Communication

Contents

Introduction

Do As I Say is a photocopyable collection of three kinds of sequential activities: operations, procedures, and rituals. For simplicity, we will refer to them as sequences. The collection includes sequences that can be used with beginning, intermediate, and advanced students. They can be used with young and old learners. The sequences are typically done as pairwork.

What Are Operations, Procedures, and Rituals?

They all have one thing in common: a series of steps that follow a logical and/or naturally occurring sequence. They differ from each other in this way: An **operation** involves manipulating a piece of equipment, such as operating a tape recorder. A **procedure** is an activity that follows a predictable series of steps such as preparing a cup of instant coffee or a more complex activity such as making origami. A **ritual** is a highly predictable conversational dialogue.

Language accompanies each step in the sequence. Typically, the language is a short sentence, usually a command to do something or a cue to say something. The accurate use of language leads the learner through the process of successfully completing the sequence of steps. For example, Student A gives directions to Student B, and unless those directions are correct and correctly followed, Student B will not or should not successfully complete the sequence. Language accompanies action and/or thought. The meaning of the language is made clear by the action, and the action reinforces the language. The experience of completing a sequence establishes a basis for tactile and visual memory as well as linguistic memory. Furthermore, learners will experience many of these sequences in their normal daily life outside the classroom, and as they are involved in the sequence, they will also be involved with the language that accompanies the sequence. The result is an effective activity for language acquisition. They are learning by doing.

The operations and procedures are usually a set of instructions delivered in the form of commands. A ritual sequence is usually a set of verbal exchanges, such as a series of questions that elicit responses. The most useful format is called the "8 by 8," a series of eight utterances, each utterance not exceeding eight words. Learners are better able to remember and work with utterances of eight or fewer words. If the sequence has more than eight steps, the learner may have more difficulty remembering the steps. In some of the more complex sequences, the lines do exceed the eight-word, eight-line limit. These sequences should be used with more advanced learners.

Introduction

The sequences are also an enjoyable way for learners to use the language actively in a purposeful way. They are fun. At the same time, the interaction between the learners is meaningful. A machine is used, or a task is accomplished. Thus, the sequences provide two important prerequisites to successful language acquisition — enjoyable and meaningful practice.

Because the sequences involve action, they are especially useful for the acquisition of the verb phrase — the heart of the language. The verbs used in the sequences are characteristically high-frequency action verbs, often irregular, for example, *put, hold, open, close, give,* and *take.* Sequences also feature phrasal verbs such as *turn on, pick up, fill in* and *write down.* With a few simple cues, a variety of tenses can be practiced. For example, at the end of each step, the question "What did you do?" will require the learner to use past tense forms.

Sequences also add variety to the usual classroom activities, and variety keeps the students on their toes. At the same time, the teacher can withdraw from direct participation in the sequence, allowing the learners to perform and practice by themselves, reducing teacher-talk and increasing learner-talk.

When to Use Sequences

Sequences are generally used as a supplement to a regular curriculum. For example, after working with irregular past tense forms, the teacher can select a sequence such as "Lighting a Candle" that uses several irregular verbs and requires the learners to ask "What did you do?" after each step. They can also be used on a regular basis to begin a class, to close it, or to break the tempo of the regular class work.

Sequences can be used at any level of English proficiency, although they are more effective at beginning and intermediate levels. There are six categories of sequences in this collection, and within each category, the sequences become progressively more challenging.

Reviewing and recycling material has always been an important part of any effective language learning program, and doing sequences is no exception. Therefore, "once is never enough" is a good rule to follow with these sequences. Frequently, a brief announcement such as "Let's mail a letter" is all that is needed to set a sequence in motion, and with each review, a different tense can be used, for example, "Before you do it, say what you are going to do."

How to Use Sequences

As noted previously, this collection is copyable. There are usually two sequences per page, frequently related to each other. The page can be copied, cut, and a sequence given to each pair of students — or each student. The sequences can also be pasted on 5x7 index cards, and to make them last even longer, laminated.

Part Two of the book includes teaching notes, and although the sequences can be used in a variety of ways, **a basic procedure with variations is outlined below.**

A. Speak, Listen, and Respond by Doing

1. Introduce the sequence. Go through it completely once to give the learners a general idea of what it's about. Demonstrate each step with any appropriate actions.

2. Hand out the sequence and go through it again with the learners following along reading, as well as listening.

3. Clarify any vocabulary problems.

4. Go through the sequence again with the students repeating in unison.

5. Pair the students and have them go through the sequence, referring to the handout as necessary. They take turns speaking and responding.

6. Have the students do it again without referring to their handouts.

7. *(optional)* Have the pairs split up, find a new partner and do it again.

8. *(optional)* Have volunteers perform the sequence for others.

B. Tense Variations

By introducing the following questions into the sequence, have the students practice a variety of verb tenses.

> **Present Progressive**
> A: Walk to the door
> B: (starts walking)
> A: (while the student is walking) What are you doing?
> B: I'm walking to the door.

How to Use Sequences

Simple Past

    A: Open the door.
    B: (opens the door)
    A: What did you do?
    B: I opened the door.

Going to Future

    A: Close the window. Wait! What are you going to do?
    B: I'm going to close the window.

Will Future

    A: (after completing the sequence)
       If you do this again tomorrow, what will you do?
    B: I'll put the pencil in the sharpener. Then I'll hold it
       firmly and turn the crank, etc.

Present Perfect

    A: Thread the needle.
    B: (threads the needle)
    A: Good! What have you just done?
    B: I've just threaded the needle.

    A: (After several steps). What have you done so far/ up to now?
    B: I've put the plate in the center of the placemat. I've folded the
       napkin and put it to the left of the plate, etc.

Past Progressive

    A: Write your name on the board.
    B: (starts writing)
    A: Stop! . . What were you doing when I told you to stop?
    B: I was writing my name.

Simple Present

    A: (after completing a sequence) What do you do when you pot a plant?
    B: Well, I (or you) put some stones into a pot. Then I (or you) fill the pot
       half full of soil, etc.

C. Person and Number Variations

In addition to the usual first person "I" and second person singular "you," have the students work in groups of three to work on **third person singular**.

> A: Set the clock to the correct time.
> B: (starts to set the clock)
> A: What is she doing?
> C: She's setting the clock.

Have groups of four work on first, second, and third plural person

> A: Stand up very slowly. What are you (B & C) doing?
> B & C: We're standing up.
> A: What are they doing?
> D: They're standing up.

D. General Suggestions

1. Some of the sequences may need adjustment to fit your own situation. So, make your own adaptation of the sequence.

2. Encourage the use of discourse connectors: *first, then, next, before, after that,* etc.

3. Have the students write the sequence after they have done it.

4. Give the sequence as a dictation, rather than giving it to the students as a handout.

5. Have a student mime a sequence as others describe what is happening.

6. Ask the students to create their own personal sequences:

> *Before class I . .*
> *After class I . .*
> *Every Sunday I . . .*
> *When I go to X, I . . .*

How to Use Sequences

7. With some of the sequences, modal verb phrases can be used:

    A: <u>Can</u> you jump on one leg?
    B: Yes, I can.
    A: Go ahead.
    B: (jumps)

    A: What do you <u>have to</u> do in order to set a table?
    B: First you have to . . . etc.

    A: Would you please . . .

See page 50

1.1 Following Directions

1. Say this word: _____

2. Repeat it.

3. Ask me to spell it.

4. Listen carefully. __ __ __ __ __ __ __

5. Answer my question: How do you spell it?

6. Now write the word.

7. Read it to me.

See page 50

1.2 Asking Permission

1. Raise your hand.

2. Ask to leave the room.   May I leave the room?

3. Go to the door.

4. Go out of the room.

5. Come back to the door.

6. Ask to come in.   May I come in?

7. Come back to your seat.

See page 50

1.3 Drawing a Picture

1. Draw a lake.

2. Draw two trees next to the lake.

3. Draw a rock between the trees.

4. Draw a boat on the lake.

5. Draw the sun over the lake.

6. Draw two birds near the trees.

7. Draw grass around the lake.

See page 51

1.4 Coloring the Picture

1. Color the lake blue.

2. Color the trees green and brown.

3. Draw a frog on the rock.

4. Color the frog green.

5. Do not color the boat.

6. Color the sun yellow.

7. Do not color the birds.

8. Color the grass green.

See page 51

1.5 Playing with Numbers

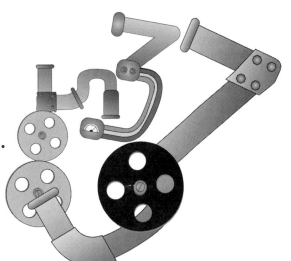

1. Add 5, 7, and 3.

2, Remember the sum.

3. Subtract 5 from the sum.

4. Multiply by 7.

5. Divide by 2.

6. Add 5 to the total.

7. Write down the number.

See page 51

1.6 Using a Calculator

1. Turn the calculator on.

2. Press 9, the addition sign, 8, and the equals sign.

3. Press the subtraction sign, 9, and the equals sign.

4. Press eight, the multiplication sign, and the equals sign.

5. Say the answer.

6. Press the clear button.

7. Turn the calculator off.

Do As I Say

See page 52

1.7 Using a Board

1. Go to the board.

2. Pick up a (marker/piece of chalk).

3. Write your name on the board.

4. Put the (marker/piece of chalk) back.

5. Pick up an eraser.

6. Erase your name.

7. Put the eraser back.

8. Go back to your seat.

See page 52

1.8 Giving Classroom Instructions

1. Open/close the door.

2. Lock/unlock the door.

3. Turn on/turn off the lights.

4. Turn up/turn down the thermostat.

5. Open/close a window.

6. Pull up/pull down a shade.

7. Write on/erase the board.

8. Take out/put away your textbook.

g.

c.

d.

f.

e.

b.

h.

a.

See page 52

1.9 Sharpening a Pencil

1. Pick up and hold the pencil.

2. Put the end of the pencil into the hole in the pencil sharpener.

3. Hold the pencil firmly.

4. Turn the crank.

5. Keep turning the crank until the pencil is sharp.

6. Take the pencil out.

7. Look to see if it is sharp.

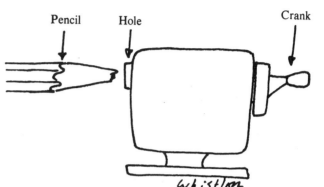

Pencil Hole Crank

whistlon

See page 53

1.10 Operating a Cassette Recorder

1. Plug in the recorder (or check the batteries).

2. Push the eject button to open the recorder.

3. Insert a cassette and close the cover.

4. Push the fast forward button to advance the tape and then push stop.

5. Push the play and record buttons to record.

6. Say something.

7. Push the stop button.

8. Push the rewind button to rewind the tape.

9. Push the play button to listen.

See page 53

1.11 Playing a Number Game

1. Take this piece of paper.

2. Get a pen or pencil.

3. Write three numbers on the paper.
   Use only one to ten.

4. Remember the number.

5. Fold the paper in half.

6. Give it to _____.

7. Listen for your number.

See page 53

1.12 Playing Bingo

1. Write 25 numbers in the squares.
   Use only the numbers on the Bingo card.

2. Raise your hand when you are ready.

3. Listen to the caller.

4. Look for the number in the letter column.

5. If you have the letter and number, mark the square.

6. Say "Bingo!" when you have a complete line.

7. Read your line.

B I N G O

Bingo Numbers

10 11 12 13 14 15 16 17 18 19

20 30 40 50 60 70 80 90

33 44 55 66 77 88 99

See page 54

1.13 Using a Dictionary

1. Look at the first letter of the word.

2. Open the dictionary.

3. Find the section with the first letter of the word.

4. Look at the second letter of the word.

5. Find the words starting with those letters.

6. Look at the words at the top of the page.

7. Find the right page for your word.

8. Find your word and read the definition.

See page 54

1.14 Looking Up a Word

1. Look up the word _____.

2. Count the number of syllables.

3. Find the stressed syllable.

4. Pronounce it.

5. Tell what part of speech it is.

6. Tell how many meanings it has.

7. Read the first meaning.

See page 55

1.15 Meeting Someone

A. Tomorrow let's go to _____.

B. Good idea. What time?

A: How about _____ o'clock?

B: I'm busy at _____ o'clock.

A: How about _____ o'clock.

B: Sounds good.

A: See you there.

B: See you.

See page 55

1.16 Practicing Politeness

A: Excuse me.

B: Sure, What can I do for you?

A: I'm sorry to bother you.

B: No problem.

A: Would you mind holding this for a minute?

B: No, not at all.

A: Would you mind if I also gave you this?

B: No, I don't mind.

A: Thank you. I'll be back in a minute.

See page 55

1.17 Apologizing

A: Sorry to keep you waiting.

B: That's OK. You don't need to apologize.
   Here are your things.

A: Thank you.

B: No problem.

A: Uhm. Could you do me a favor?

B: I guess so. What is it?

A: Can I borrow your _____.

See page 56

1.18 Reminding Politely

B: Do you still have my _____?

A: What do you mean?

B: I lent you my _____.

A: Oh, yes. I'm glad you reminded me.

B: Would you be able to return it?

A: Of course. Here it is.

B: Thank you.

A: Thank YOU.

Classroom Activities

See page 56

1.19 Making a Paper Hat

1. Fold the paper in half with the folded edge up.

2. Fold the paper in half from left to right.

3. Unfold the paper once, leaving a line down the center and a fold at the top.

4. Bring the top right corner to the center line.

5. Bring the top left corner to the center line.

6. Fold the top sheet of the bottom rectangular piece up.

7. Turn the hat over.

8. Fold the other bottom piece up.

See page 57

1.20 Making a Paper Airplane

1. Fold a sheet of paper in half lengthwise with the folded edge down.

2. Bring one top edge down to the crease and fold.

3. Turn over and repeat on the othe side.

4. Fold again, bringing the upper folded corner, Point A, down to point B and crease the paper.

5. Repeat on the other side.

6. Make a lengthwise fold to make a wing.

7. Make another wing on the other side.

8. Fly the airplane to test it.

Classroom Activities

Do As I Say

See page 57

1.21 Making an Origami Cicada

1. Fold square ABCD diagonally along line DB.

2. Bring points B and D to point A (C), folding along lines XY and ZY.

3. Fold point D down near point Y along line XQ.

4. Do the same for point B on the other side by folding along QZ.

5. Folding along the line RS, bring point C down to cover point Q.

6. Fold line RS down past line XZ, but not past point C.

7. Fold points X and Z behind along lines MN and OP.

8. Fold point A behind along line TU.

9. Fold points T and U back to make the cicada's eyes.

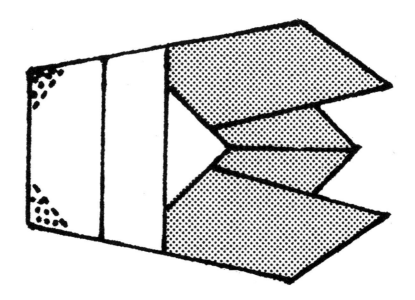

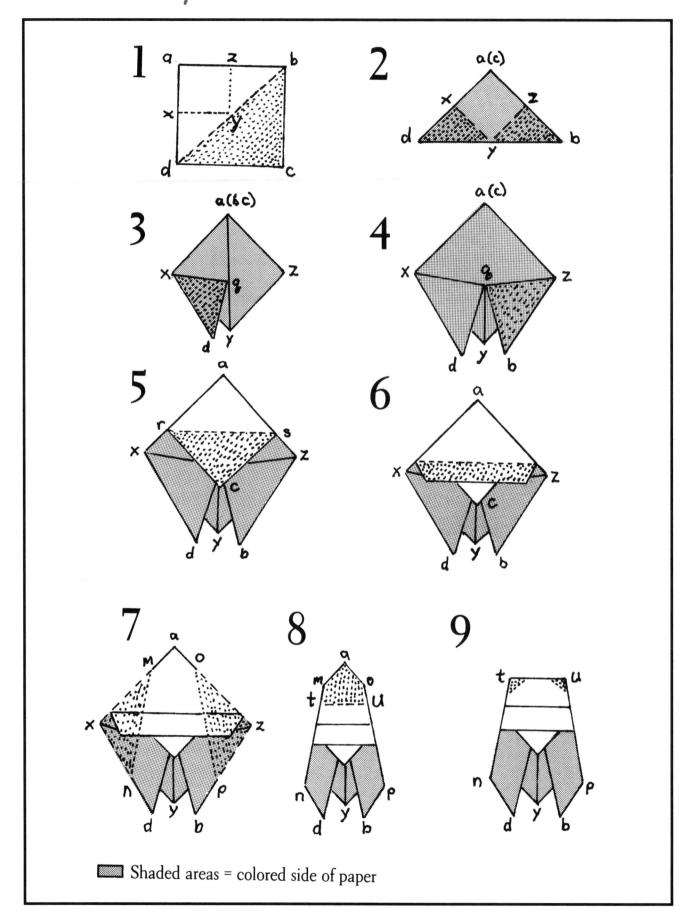

Shaded areas = colored side of paper

Household Activities
Do As I Say

See page 58

2.1 Lighting a Candle

1. Open the matchbox.

2. Take out a match.

3. Close the matchbox.

4. Strike the match.

5. Hold the flame to the candle wick.

6. Light the candle.

7. Blow out the match.

8. Throw away the match.

See page 58

2.2 Setting a Table

1. Put the plate in the center of the placemat.

2. Fold the napkin.

3. Put the napkin to the left of the plate.

4. Place the knife to the right of the plate.

5. Put the teaspoon to the right of the knife.

6. Put the fork on the left-hand side of the plate, on top of the napkin.

7. Set the glass near the tip of the knife.

See page 58

2.3 Setting a Clock Radio Alarm

1. Set the clock to the correct time.

2. Decide the time you want for the alarm.

3. Use the alarm set control.

4. Set the hour for a.m.

5. Set the minute.

6. Select radio or alarm.

7. When the alarm sounds, turn it off.

8. Don't go back to sleep. Get up.

See page 59

2.4 Washing Dishes

1. Scrape and rinse the dishes.

2. Fill the dishpan with water.

3. Add the detergent.

4. Put some dishes in the dishpan.

5. Scrub the dishes clean.

6. Rinse the clean dishes.

7. Put the dishes in the drainer to dry.

8. When the dishes are dry, put them away.

See page 59

2.5 Threading a Needle

1. Hold the needle between your thumb and first finger.

2. Hold the thread in your other hand.

3. Moisten one end of the thread with your mouth.

4. Put the thread through the eye of the needle.

5. Pull the thread through.

6. Tie a knot in one end of the thread.

7. Make the knotted end longer than the other end.

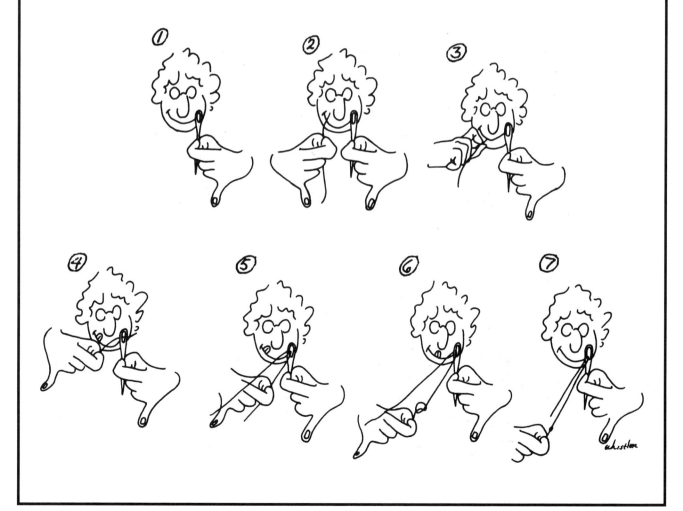

See page 60

2.6 Sewing on a Button

1. Thread the needle.

2. Tie a knot in the end of the thread.

3. Hold the button on the fabric.

4. Pull the needle through the fabric and one of the holes in the button.

5. Bring the needle back through another hole.

6. Repeat until the button is on tight.

7. Tie a knot in the thread.

8. Cut the thread.

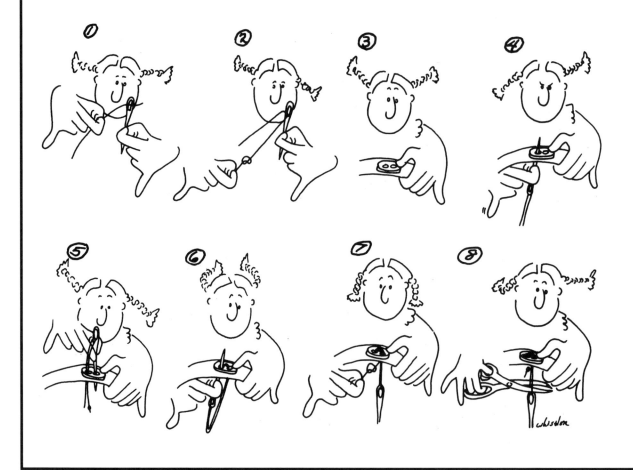

See page 60

2.7 Pounding a Nail

1. Pick up the nail with one hand.

2. Hold it between your thumb and first finger.

3. Pick up the hammer with your other hand.

4. Hold it at the end of the handle.

5. Put the sharp end of the nail against the wood.

6. Hit the head of the nail with the hammer.

7. Remove your fingers when the nail is secure.

8. Continue hitting the head until the nail is hammered into the wood.

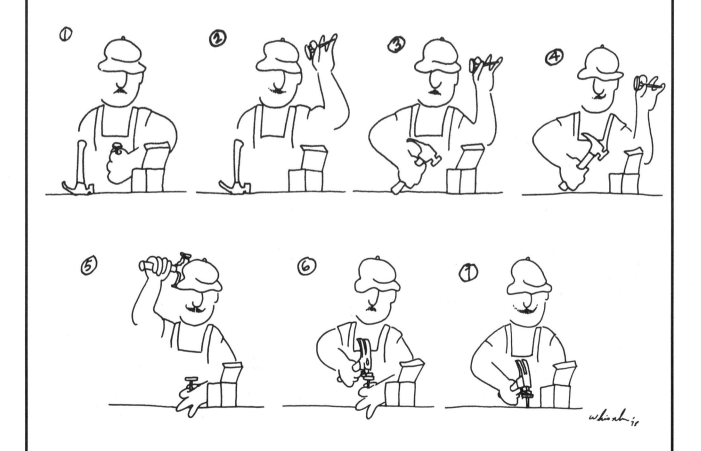

See page 61

2.8 Potting a Plant

1. Put some stones gently into the pot.

2. Fill the pot half full with soil.

3. Place the plant firmly into the soil.

4. Fill the pot up carefully with soil.

5. Press the soil firmly around the plant.

6. Water the plant slowly.

7. Let the excess water drain out of the pot.

See page 61

2.9 Changing Batteries in a Flashlight

1. Unscrew the flashlight.

2. Dump the old batteries into your hand.

3. Put them aside.

4. Find the positive (+) and negative (–) signs on the new batteries.

5. Put the two new batteries into the flashlight with the postive ends toward the bulb.

6. Screw the flashlight back together.

7. Turn the flashlight on to make sure that it works.

8. Throw the old batteries away.

Household Activities

Do As I Say

See page 62

2.10 Greeting a Guest

A: (Knocks on the door)

B: (Opens door) Hello. It's good to see you.

A: Good to see you.

B: Come on in.

A: Thanks.

B: How have you been?

A: Fine thanks, and you?

B: Just fine. Come and say hello to _____.

See page 62

2.11 Taking Leave

A: Well, I think it's time to go.

B: Really? Do you have to?

A: I'm afraid so. But I've enjoyed the visit very much.

B: That's good. So have I.

A: We'll have to get together again.

B: Good idea.

A: Next time you'll have to come to my place.

B: Well, thanks for coming.

A: And thank you for inviting me.

See page 63

3.1 Blowing up a Balloon

1. Stretch the balloon.

2. Put the open end to your lips.

3. Blow up the balloon until it's full of air.

4. Take it away from your lips.

5. Hold the end tight so the air doesn't escape.

6. Tie a knot in the end of the balloon.

See page 63

3.2 Hopping on One Leg

1. Stand with both feet one foot apart.

2. Bend your left knee.

3. Raise your left foot behind you.

4. Grab your left ankle with your left hand.

5. Hop five times.

6. Let go of your ankle.

7. Put your foot back on the floor.

See page 63

3.3 Touching Your Toes

1. Stand up.

2. Place your feet a foot apart.

3. Raise your arms up over your head.

4. Bend down from the waist and . . .

5. Touch your toes with your fingers.

6. Keep your knees straight.

7. Straighten up and bring your hands to your waist.

8. Drop your hands to your sides.

See page 64

3.4 Doing Jumping Jacks

1. Stand up straight with your arms to your sides.

2. Swing both legs out to the side and . .

3. At the same time swing your arms out and . . .

4. Touch your hands up over your head.

5. Then bring your feet back together and . . .

6. Bring your arms back down to your side.

7. Do it again . . .and again. . . and again. . .

See page 64

3.5 Playing Jacks

1. Throw the jacks onto the floor.

2. Toss the ball into the air.

3. Pick up one jack before the ball bounces.

4. Let the ball bounce once.

5. Catch the ball with the same hand.

6. Put the jack into the other hand.

7. Repeat until you've picked up all the jacks, one at a time.

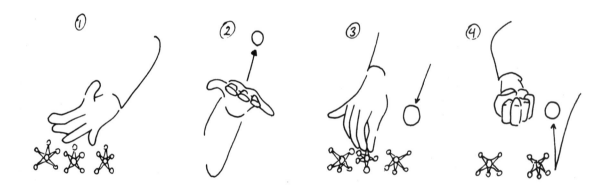

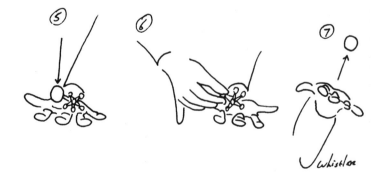

Games and Exercises

See page 65

3.6 Playing Dice

1. Pick up two dice.

2. Throw the dice on top of the table.

3. Count the number of dots on top of the dice.

4. Put a check mark after the same number on the score sheet.

5. Give the dice to the next player.

6. Tell them to do the same thing.

7. Continue until you have checked all the numbers.

Score Sheet	
2	
3	
4	
5	
6	
7	
8	
9	
10	
11	
12	

6	
7	
8	✔

Check mark

See page 65

3.7 Setting up a Chessboard

1. Set up the board with the white square in the lower right-hand corner.

2. Place the castles on each corner square.

3. Put the knights next to the castles.

4. Position the bishops beside the knights.

5. Locate the queen on the white square next to a bishop.

6. Set the king on the black square between the queen and the bishop.

7. Place the pawns in a row on the squares in front of the other pieces.

Games and Exercises

See page 66

3.8 Would You Please

A: Would you mind touching the floor?

B: (touches the floor)

A: Would you please jump up and down three times?

B: (jumps)

A: Would you please turn around?

B: (turns around)

A: Now touch your toes.

B: (does not touch their toes)

See page 66

3.9 Negotiating an Invitation

A: Let's play _____.
B: I'd rather not.
A: Why not?
B: I don't know how.
   I don't feel like it.
A: Then how about _____?
B: That sounds OK.
A: Good. Let's play.

Monopoly, checkers, chess, Chinese checkers,
backgammon, Parcheesi, go fish, hearts, poker,
bingo, tennis, golf, Ping Pong, pool, darts,
charades, twenty questions, Jeopardy

Food and Recipes

See page 67

4.1 Eating a Banana

1. Peel back the banana skin from the top end.
2. Take a bite out of the banana.
3. Chew it up and swallow it.
4. Continue peeling and eating.
5. Throw away the peel . .
6. . . . but don't throw it on the ground.
7. Find a wastebasket.
8. Put it in the wastebasket.

See page 67

4.2 Making a Cup of Tea

1. Boil some water.
2. Put a tea bag in the cup.
3. Pour boiling water into the cup.
4. Let the tea steep.
5. Remove the tea bag.
6. If you want to, add some milk.
7. If you want to, add some sugar.
8. Stir and sip.

See page 68

4.3 Making Instant Pudding

1. Read the directions on the package.

2. Open the package and pour the contents into a bowl.

3. Add the correct amount of milk.

4. Stir the mixture together.

5. Pour it into bowls.

6. Allow it to thicken.

7. Enjoy it.

See page 68

4.4 Making a Peanut Butter and Jelly Sandwich

1. Take two slices of bread from the package.

2. Unscrew the lid of the peanut butter jar.

3. Unscrew the lid of the jelly jar.

4. Spread the peanut butter on one slice of bread.

5. Spread the jelly on the other slice of bread.

6. Put the two slices of bread together.

7. Cut the sandwich in half.

8. Screw the lids onto the jars.

See page 69

4.5 Making Spaghetti

1. Read the directions on the spaghetti box.

2. Fill the pan almost full of water.

3. Turn the burner on high.

4. Wait for the water to boil.

5. Put in the spaghetti.

6. Let it boil for as long as the directions say.

7. Test the spaghetti for softness.

8. If it's ready, pour it into a colander.

See page 69

4.6 Eating Spaghetti

1. Use tongs to serve a dish full of spaghetti.

2. Put some spaghetti sauce on top.

3. Sprinkle some grated cheese on top of the sauce.

4. Let the spaghetti cool off a little.

5. Twirl some spaghetti around a fork.

6. Eat the spaghetti.

7. Take another mouthful.

See page 70

4.7 Making a Cup of Instant Coffee

1. Boil some water.

2. Put some instant coffee into a cup.

3. Fill the cup with boiling water.

4. Stir the coffee.

5. If you want to, add some milk.

6. If you want to, add some sugar.

7. Stir the coffee again.

See page 70

4.8 Making Coffee with a Coffeemaker

1. Open the door of the coffeemaker.

2. Put a coffee filter around the inside of the basket.

3. Put three scoops of coffee into the filter
   to make six cups of coffee.

4. Close the door.

5. Take out the glass pot.

6. Fill the pot with cold water to the six-cup mark.

7. Open the top of the coffee maker and pour in the water.

8. Turn the coffeemaker on.

See page 71

4.9 Ordering a Cup of Coffee

A: May I help you?

B: I'd like a cup of coffee.

A: Regular or decaf?

B: _____, please.

A: Cream and sugar or sweetener?

B: _____, please.

A: Anything else?

B: No, that's all.

See page 71

4.10 Making Popcorn

1. Put the correct amount of popcorn into a measuring cup.

2. Pour the popcorn into the popper.

3. Plug in the popper.

4. While you wait, melt some butter.

5. When the popping has stopped, unplug the popper.

6. Pour the popcorn into a bowl.

7. Pour the butter over the popcorn.

8. Sprinkle some salt on the popcorn.

See page 72

4.11 Ordering a Pizza for Delivery

1. Call a pizza place.
2. Tell the size and type
   of pizza that you want.
3. Order any special toppings.
4. Specify delivery.
5. Give your address
   and the phone number.
6. Give directions if necessary.
7. Ask how much it will be.

small
medium
large

thin crust
deep dish

black olives
sausage
pepperoni
mushrooms
onion
green pepper

See page 72

4.12 Using a Fast Food Drive-Through

1. Drive to the speaker at the menu sign.
2. Open your window.
3. Wait for a voice.
4. Order your food.
5. Drive to the pick-up window.
6. Pay for the food.
7. Take the change and the food.
8. Roll up the window and drive away.

Food and Recipes

See page 73

4.13 Eating in a Restaurant

A: Hello, my name is _____. I'll be your server.

B: Hello.

A: Our specials today are _____. Can I get you something to drink?

C: Yes, I'll have _____.

A: Here are your drinks. Are you ready to order?

B: I'd like to have _____.

A: Anything else?

C: Not now, thank you.

See page 73

4.14 Shopping in a Supermarket

1. Get a shopping cart.

2. Check your shopping list.

3. Wheel the cart up and down the aisles.

4. Get the items that you need and check them off the list.

5. Go to a check-out line.

6. Put your groceries on the belt.

7. Pay for your purchases.

8. Take your receipt and change.

See page 74

5.1 Mailing a Letter

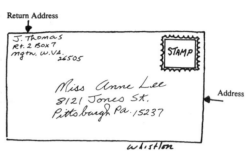

1. Fold the letter to fit the envelope.

2. Insert the letter in the envelope.

3. Lick the flap and seal the envelope.

4, Write the address on the front of the envelope.

5. Write the return address in the upper left-hand corner.

6. If necessary, lick the stamp.

7. Put the stamp in the upper right-hand corner.

8. Mail the letter.

See page 74

5.2 Buying Stamps

A: Next, please. Can I help you?

B: Yes. I'd like to buy some stamps.

A: First class letters are _____ cents. Is that what you want?

B: Yes. I need _____.

A: That'll be _____.

B: May I have a receipt, please?

A: Of course. Here you are.

B: Thank you.

A: Next, please.

See page 75

5.3 Using a Pay Telephone

1. Read the directions.

2. Pick up the telephone receiver.

3. Hold it to your ear.

4. Insert the correct amount of money.

5. Listen for the dial tone.

6. Press the keys for the number that you are calling.

7. Listen until someone on the other end answers.

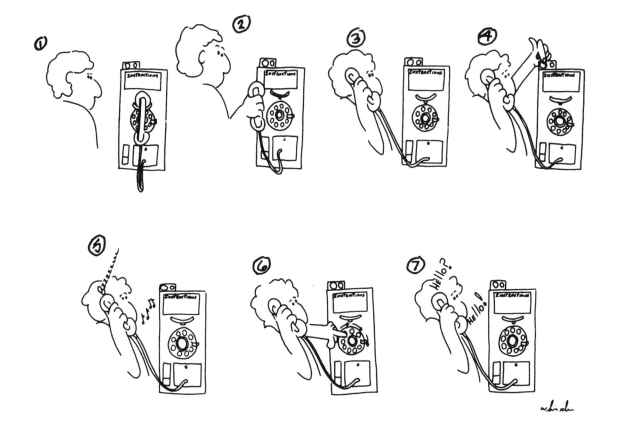

See page 75

5.4 Leaving a Message

1. Listen to the recorded message.

2. After the signal, begin speaking.

3. Give your name and phone number.

4. Leave your message.

5. When you finish your message, leave any instructions.

6. End your recording with "That's all, thank you."

7. Hang up the phone.

SAMPLE RECORDED MESSAGES

Hello, This is _____. We're not at home. Please leave a message after the tone and we'll call back.

_____

This is the _____ Company. We're either on the phone or out of the office. Your call is important to us, so please leave your name and phone number, and we'll get back to you.

See page 75

5.5 Using a Prepaid Phone Card

1. Look at the instructions on the back of the card.

2. Dial the 800 number.

3. Enter the PIN number.

4. Listen for the amount of time remaining on your card.

5. Dial the number you want to call.

6. Talk to the person who answers or leave a message.

7. Hang up the phone.

SAMPLE PHONE CARD

| From USA | ***ESL FONCO*** | 60 US minutes |

1. Dial 1-800-123-7899

2. Enter PIN Number   88899-17745

3. Follow voice prompts for dialing instructions.

For calls from overseas to USA dial Country specific Toll-Free number, then use World Service Code 72.

By using this card, you accept the terms of ESL FONCO. For problems or assistance, dial 1-800-321- 7779. Card expires 15 months from activation date. Pay phones have an additional 50¢ surcharge.

See page 76

5.6 Wiring Money

1. Tell the person at the desk that you want to wire some money.
2. Fill out the money order form.
3. Print clearly and carefully.
4. Hand in the completed form.
5. Pay for the money order and the service charge.
6. Get a receipt for your money order.

$ WorldWide CashWire

To send money
Form 483g

Customer Number ☐☐☐☐☐

☐ Sending money to U.S.A.
☐ International CashWire

Expected payout location
Address   City   Country

Dollar amount in words

If the receiver does not have proper identification and the amount of the cash wire is less than $1,000, the receiver may be given the money if the following test question is answered correctly.

Dollar amount in numbers $

When sending $1,000 or more, you must provide proper identification and additional information.

Question *(8 words or less)*

Answer required

Receiver

Sender's name   First name   Middle name   Family name

Optional services available at additional cost. Check the desired services.

Sender's address   Street number and name/Post Office Box

☐ Deliver a check to the following address

City   State   Zip Code

☐ Telephone this number to say the CashWire has arrived. (   )

Sender's Telephone
(   )

☐ Include this message:

Customer's signature   Date

See page 76

5.7 Receiving an Email

1. Turn on the computer.

2. Double click on mail.

3. Click on send and receive.

4. Check your in-box for new messages.

5. Select a message to read.

6. Decide if you want to delete or answer it.

7. If you want to answer, decide if you want to reply or compose a new message.

See page 77

5.8 Using a FAX Machine

1. Look over the message to be faxed to be sure it's ready.
2. Feed the paper face-down into the machine.
3. Press the button marked "_____."
4. Punch in the number you are calling.
5. Check the display to be sure it is correct.

6. If it is correct, press the button marked "_____"

7. Listen fror the sound called the electronic handshake.

8. Press the key marked "report" to see if your message was received.

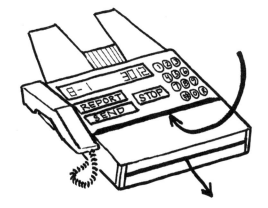

See page 77

5.9 Making a Plane Reservation on the Web

1. Go to a travel or airline web site.

2. Click on reservations or schedule.

3. Select your departure city and departure day.

4. Select the arrival city and arrival day.

5. Review the itineraries.

6. Choose an itinerary.

7. Purchase the ticket.

See page 77

5.10 Searching the Internet

1. Turn on the computer.

2. Double click on "Browse the Internet"

3. Choose a search engine.

4. Type in a key word or phrase for the subject of your search.

5. Click on "go."

6. Review the search results.

7. Check out web sites that seem useful.

See page 78

6.1 Writing a Check

1. Write today's date in ink on the date line.

2. Write the payee's name on the next line.

3. Write the amount of the check in figures.

4. Write the amount of the check in words.

5. Sign the check on the last line.

6. Make a note on the memo line.

7. Record the transaction in your check register.

ROBERT A. TAFT	No. 122	
1958 SENATOR ROW		
TAFTSTOWN, OHIO 43216	_____ 19 _____	59-7263/2115

PAY TO THE ORDER OF _____ $ [   ]

_____ DOLLARS

Croesus National Bank
MEMBER FDIC
BOOSTERVILLE, OHIO 43227

Memo _____ _____

⑆211572631⑆ 05 40 013007⑈ 0122

CHECK REGISTER RECORDS

RECORD ALL CHARGES OR CREDITS THAT AFFECT YOUR ACCOUNT

NUMBER	DATE	TRANSACTION DECRIPTION OR PAYEE NAME	(−) PAYMENT OR WITHDRAWAL		(+) DEPOSIT OR INTEREST	BALANCE $	

See page 78

6.2 Using a Vending Machine

1. Read the directions on the machine.

2. Select what you want to buy.

3. Find the money slot.

4. Insert the money.

5. Push the button for your selection.

6. Open the door or pull the knob.

7. Take your selection from the machine.

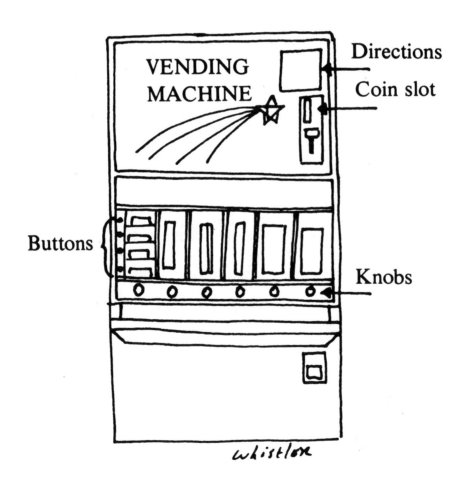

See page 79

6.3 Filling in a Form

1. Read the directions at the top of the form.

2. Write your name — last name first.

3. Enter your address.

4. Give your date of birth.

5. Check your marital status and educational level.

6. Write in your social security and driver's license numbers.

7. Sign the form.

8. Write today's date.

See page 79

6.4 Using an ATM Card to Withdraw from Checking

1. Read the directions.
2. Put your card into the slot.
3. Punch in your personal identification number (PIN).

4. Select "Withdrawal from Checking."
5. Enter the amount you want to withdraw.
6. Remove the money.
7. Take your card.

APPLICATION

INSTRUCTIONS: Fill out this application completely. Do not omit any answers.
Print your responses in capital letters (ABCDEF, etc.).

NAME _____

      (Last)   (First)   (Middle)

ADDRESS

_____

(Number and street)

_____ _____

     (City)   (State/Province)

_____ _____

   (Zip)   (Country)

MARITAL STATUS
_____ Single
_____ Married
_____ Widowed

EDUCATIONAL LEVEL
_____ Secondary
_____ AA Degree
_____ BA Degree
_____ MA Degree
_____ Ph D
_____ Other _____

DATE OF BIRTH _____ _____ _____

              (Month)   (Day)   (Year)

SOCIAL SECURITY NUMBER _____ _____ _____

DRIVER'S LICENSE NUMBER _____ STATE _____

_____ _____

SIGNATURE   DATE

Form PLA 1348VPR-12

See page 79

6.5 Renting a DVD

1. Browse through the display racks.

2. Make a selection.

3. Bring it to the check-out desk.

4. Give your membership number.

5. Show an ID.

6. Sign the receipt.

7. Take the DVD and leave.

See page 80

6.6 Finding an Apartment

1. Find the classified ads section in the newspaper.

2. Find the "Apartments to Rent" section.

3. Decide on "furnished" or "unfurnished."

4. Read the listings.

5. Select a listing and call.

6. Ask if it's available.

7. Get more information.

8. If it sounds good, make an appointment to see it.

See page 80

6.7 Using a Laundromat

1. Open the door of the washing machine.

2. Put your clothes into the machine.

3. Select the water temperature and load size.

4. Put in the soap.

5. Close the door.

6. Put the correct amount of money into the machine.

7. When the machine has finished, remove your clothes and take them to a dryer.

See page 80

6.8 Using a Self-Service Gas Pump

1. Drive up to a self-serve pump.

2. Remove your gas cap.

3. Choose your payment option.

4. Select the grade of gas that you want.

5. Put the nozzle into the gas tank.

6. Squeeze the handle on the nozzle.

7. Release the handle when you are finished.

8. Return the hose and pay for the gas.

See page 81

6.9 Starting a Car

1. Open the door and get in.

2. Fasten the seat belt.

3. Be sure the car is in park.

4. Insert the key.

5. Turn the key and step easily on the gas pedal.

6. Release the hand brake.

7. Shift into drive and step on the gas.

See page 81

6.10 Checking in at the Airport

1. Find your airline check-in counter.

2. Stand in line.

3. When it's your turn go to the counter.

4. Give the representative your ticket and ID.

5. Place your luggage on the scale.

6. Take your boarding pass and go to security.

7. Pass through security.

8. Find your gate.

Classroom Activities

1.1 Following Directions *(Page 1)*

MATERIALS: Several words on individual slips of paper

GRAMMAR AND VOCABULARY:

- Personal pronouns: *me* (direct object) *to me* (indirect object) *my*
- *It* as direct object referent

NOTES:

1. The verbs in this sequence are typical classroom instruction commands. So this could be a good procedure to use right at the beginning of the course.
2. The respondent does have some words to say and one line, *"Please spell it."* You may have to put the line on the board or dictate it.
3. The activity involves oral spelling. You may need to work on it before doing the sequence.

1.2 Asking Permission *(Page 1)*

MATERIALS: None

GRAMMAR AND VOCABULARY:

1. Prepositional phrases: *to the door,* etc.
2. Phrasal verb: *come back*
3. Modal for permission: *may*

NOTES:

This activity may require your participation as the students ask for permission to leave. You can have another student act as your stand-in

1.3 Drawing a Picture *(Page 2)*

MATERIALS: Paper, pens or pencils

GRAMMAR AND VOCABULARY:

- Locative prepositional phrases: *next to,* etc.
- Count and non-count nouns: *two trees, grass*
- Definite and indefinite articles: *a lake, the sun*

NOTES:

1. With only one verb, this should be an easy activity.
2. Do it again later with a different scene. ex: the student's house.
3. Post all the pictures to see the variations and individuality.

Teaching Notes

1.4 Coloring the Picture (Page 2)

MATERIALS The picture from the previous activity. Crayons

GRAMMAR AND VOCABULARY:

    1. shift from *a* to *the*
    2. Negative imperative *do not*

NOTES:

    1. Practice with the contraction *don't*.
    2. Combine 1.3 and 1.4, and have the students create different scenes.

1.5 Playing with Numbers (Page 3)

MATERIALS: Paper, pencils

GRAMMAR:

    Verb-preposition combinations: *subtract from, multiply by*

NOTES

    1. Arithmetic words are practiced.
    2. You give the directions and the entire class follows. Then compare answers.
    3. Have the students create other arithmetic problems.

1.6 Using a Calculator (Page 3)

MATERIALS: Several calculators

GRAMMAR AND VOCABULARY:

    1. Phrasal Verbs: *turn on, turn off*
    2. Compound nouns: *addition sign*, etc
    3. Infinitives: *to turn on/off, to clear*

NOTES:

    1. Start some sentences with the infinitive: *To turn it on, press*, etc.
    2. Teach *plus, minus, divided by* and have the students say simple problems.
    3. The "clear" button on many, perhaps most, caluclators is marked "on/c."
    4. Some calculators cannot be turned off but turn off automatically in time.

1.7 Using a Board *(Page 4)*

MATERIALS: Board, markers, and erasers (enough for several pairs)

GRAMMAR AND VOCABULARY:

Separable phrasals: *pick x up, put x back*

NOTES:
1. Try using the phrasals with the object in both positions: *pick up the marker./ pick the marker up.*
2. This is a good activity for using various tenses: *What are you doing? What are you going to do, What did you do?*

1.8 Giving Classroom Instructions *(Page 4)*

MATERIALS: Whatever is available

GRAMMAR AND VOCABULARY:

Phrasal verbs

NOTES
1. You may have to vary this activity according to what is available in the classroom.
2. The sequence is not critical. The actions can be done in any order.
3. A variation: *Go open and close the door and come back. Now go turn on and turn off the lights,* etc.

1.9 Sharpening a Pencil *(Page 5)*

MATERIALS: Pencils, a pencil sharpener

GRAMMAR AND VOCABULARY:

1. *Until* clause
2. Adjective with Copular BE : *the pencil is sharp*

NOTES:
1. A variation could be to use a hand-held or electric sharpener.
2. In addition to *firmly,* other adverbs could be used: *carefully, quickly, rapidly, slowly, completely.*
3. A final step could be to use the past tense: *Tell me what you did.*

Teaching Notes

1.10 Operating a Cassette Recorder *(Page 5)*

MATERIALS: Cassette recorders, tapes

GRAMMAR AND VOCABULARY:

Infinitives: *to open, to advance, to record, to rewind, to listen*

NOTES:
1. In step # 6, the students could record this or another operation.
2. A variation could be to simply listen to the tape. You could pre-record a message: *First, you <u>pushed</u> the eject button, etc. Now you <u>are listening</u>. Finally I <u>will ask</u> you to rewind.*

1.11 Playing a Number Game *(Page 6)*

MATERIALS: Several slips of paper, a box to collect the numbers

GRAMMAR AND VOCABULARY:

Imperatives for arithmetic functions, numbers

NOTES:
1. You can play this like a lottery. Each person puts a slip in a collection box, and then you or another student pulls out a "winning number." The activity can be repeated several times.
2. Use only "teens" or "Twenty, thirty, forty," etc., instead of "one to ten."

1.12 Playing Bingo *(Page 6,7)*

MATERIALS: Several copies of the Bingo card on page 7

GRAMMAR AND VOCABULARY:

Subordinate clauses with *when* and *if*

NOTES:
1. If necessary explain the game.
2. Have pairs say the procedure to each other. Then when both have filled out a card, you call out letter-number combinations.
3. You can play the game several times. You can have the students create a new card each time (this requires several copies of the card for each student).

1.13 Using a Dictionary *(Page 8)*

MATERIALS: A dictionary for each pair, a word or words to look up

GRAMMAR AND VOCABULARY:

1. Ordinal numbers: *first, second*

2. Prepositional phrase following a noun phrase: *the first letter of the word*

NOTES:

1. You can have everybody look up the same word, or you can give each pair a different word. If each pair has a different word, they can read the definitions to each other when hey have completed the procedure.

2. After doing the procedure, you can have a "race"to find the word. You announce or write a word on the board, and then they race to be the first ones to find it.

3. When you have finished, the students can write a paragraph describing what they have done.

1.14 Looking Up a Word *(Page 8)*

MATERIALS: A dictionary for each pair, a word or words to look up

GRAMMAR AND VOCABULARY:

Embedded WH clause. Compare: *Tell what part of speech <u>it is</u>* with *What part of speech <u>is it</u>?* and *Tell how many meanings <u>it has</u>* with *How many meanings <u>does it have</u>?*

NOTES:

1. You may need to precede this with some work on syllabification and stress, as well as pronunciation symbols and abbreviations for parts of speech.

2. You can have everybody look for the same word, but it may be more interesting to give each pair a different word. When they have completed the word search, they can report to each other on what they found.

1.15 Meeting Someone *(Page 9)*

MATERIALS: None

GRAMMAR AND VOCABULARY:

1. Idiomatic *how about...?*

2. Colloquial phrases replacing sentences: *Good idea, What time? Sounds good, See you there.*

NOTES:

1. The students can provide their own variations on places and times.

2. Have pairs "act out" their rituals for other pairs.

1.16 Practicing Politeness *(Page 9)*

MATERIALS: Something to "hold," (simply a book or pencil or something silly that you bring in)

GRAMMAR AND VOCABULARY:

1. Compare *Would you mind + ing* and *Would you mind if + past tense.*

2. Notice the "no" in response to the "would you mind" questions.

NOTES:

1. This ritual can be followed later with the next ritual, and the two of them combined into a longer skit.

2. Give each pair a paper bag. Then when the ritual is finished explain the meaning of "left holding the bag."

1.17 Apologizing *(Page 10)*

MATERIALS: Something to borrow

GRAMMAR AND VOCABULARY:

1. Polite expressions of apology and forgiveness

2. Interchangeable *can* and *could*

3. Other idioms: *no problem, I guess so*

NOTES:

1. This ritual is a natural follow-up to 1.16.

2. You could work on the difference between *borrow* and *lend*, changing the last line to *Could you lend me*?

1.18 Reminding Politely *(Page 10)*

MATERIALS: The "borrowed" item from 1.17

GRAMMAR AND VOCABULARY:

1. Notice *be able to* as a substitute for *can*

2. *Lend* vs. *borrow*

NOTES:

1. This is a follow-up to 1.17 and 1.18. After you have done all three, the students can put them all together as a little skit.

2. In the last line, have them practice emphasis with the final "you."

1.19 Making a Paper Hat *(Page 11)*

MATERIALS: At least two sheets of paper for each pair

GRAMMAR AND VOCABULARY:

1. Adjectives in a series: <u>top right</u> corner

2. Separation of Verb + Preposition: *fold . . .up, turn . . over*

3. Note: *fold, unfold, folded* and *a fold*

NOTES:

1. After the procedure is done, ask the students to describe what they did.

2. This procedure would work well with an occasional "What have you done so far?"

3. Unfold the hat by giving the directions in the reverse order.

4. Have the students use the illustration as cue, rather than the words.

Teaching Notes

1.20 Making a Paper Airplane *(Page 12)*

MATERIALS: At least two sheets of paper for each pair

GRAMMAR AND VOCABULARY:

1. Infinitive phrases: *to make, to test*

2. *another* vs. *the other*

NOTES:

1. Have a contest to see whose plane can fly the highest and the longest.

2. Some students may know another way to make an airplane. Let them show how.

3. Use the illustration as cue, rather than the words.

1.21 Making an Origami Cicada *(Page 13, 14)*

MATERIALS: Origami paper, the illustration

GRAMMAR AND VOCABULARY:

Adverbs of direction: *along, down, past, back, behind*

NOTES:

This procedure is challenging. Instead of doing this as Student A telling Student B, you may have them work as a team reading and following directions to make one origami.

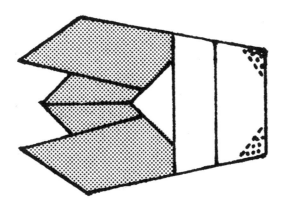

Do As I Say

Household Activities

2.1 Lighting a Candle *(Page 15)*

MATERIALS: Candles and matches

GRAMMAR AND VOCABULARY:

    Phrasal verbs: *take out, blow out, throw away*

NOTES:

    1. Do the procedure using ordinal numbers for each step.

    2. Practice with *what*. Student A asks, "What should I do first," etc.

    3. Repeat the procedure separating the two parts of the phrasal verbs.

    4. Do the procedure in the past tense. There are several irregular verbs.

2.2 Setting a Table *(Page 15)*

MATERIALS: Sets of placemats, plates, teaspoons, knives, forks, glasses, napkins

GRAMMAR AND VOCABULARY:

    Locative prepositional phrases: *in the center, to the left,* etc.

NOTES:

    1. Try doing this with the Student A saying what Student B is doing and Student B repeating. A: "Put the plate . . .She's putting the plate . ." B: "I'm putting the plate . . ."

    2. One student creates a silly place setting. She closes her eyes and describes her silly place setting to a partner, then opens her eyes to see if the partner has followed the directions correctly.

2.3 Setting a Clock Radio Alarm *(Page 16)*

MATERIALS: Clock radios

GRAMMAR AND VOCABULARY: Phrasal verbs: *turn off, go back, get up*

NOTES:

    1. Try the operation with a wind-up clock. Introduce *hour/minute hand*.

    2. Precede the operation with practice of time expressions: *ten to eight, five past eight, quarter of, etc.* When the pairs have finished, each student tells what time they set the alarm for.

2.4 Washing Dishes *(Page 16)*

MATERIALS: Dishpan, drainer, detergent, dishes

GRAMMAR AND VOCABULARY:

Subordinate clause with *when*

NOTES:

1. Repeat the procedure with future tense and more *when, before,* and *after* clauses: "<u>When</u> the dishpan is full, I will . ." "<u>Before</u> I put the dishes in the dishpan, I'm going to . . ."

2. Continue practicing subordinate clauses in the past: "After I filled the dishpan. . ."

3. This procedure can be done "dry." You can have the students go through the motions, step by step, using clean dishes without water. The steps as given in 2.4 assume you have running water. If you don't, you may want to modify the procedure.

4. Do a procedure for using an automatic dish washer.

2.5 Threading a Needle *(Page 17)*

MATERIALS: Needles, thread

GRAMMAR AND VOCABULARY:

1. Prepositional phrases: *between your thumb, with your mouth,* etc.

2. Comparative: *longer than*

NOTES:

1. Follow this procedure with 2.6 "Sewing on a Button."

2. Have the students use the illustration as cues. They can also describe what the woman in the illustration is doing.

2.6 Sewing on a Button *(Page 18)*

MATERIALS: Needles, thread, buttons, fabric, scissors

GRAMMAR AND VOCABULARY:

1. Prepositional phrases: *in the end, of the fabric,* etc.

2. *Until* clause

NOTES:

1. Use the illustration instead of the sentences.

2. Follow this with a "knitting lesson."

3. Try doing the procedure with *have got to* For example, "First you've got to (gotta) . ."

2.7 Pounding a Nail *(Page 19)*

MATERIALS: Nails, hammer, wood

GRAMMAR AND VOCABULARY:

1. Instrumental prepositional phrases: *with one hand, with the hammer*

2. Genitive prepositional phrases: *end of the handle, head of the nail*

3. Clauses with *until, when*

4. Passive voice: "the nail <u>is hammered</u>"

NOTES:

1. Do the entire procedure in the passive voice; "The nail <u>is picked up</u> . ."

2. Add adverbs: *carefully, tightly,* etc.

3. Create a similar procedure wth a saw or drill.

4. Use the illustrations instead of the sentences.

2.8 Potting a Plant *(Page 20)*

MATERIALS: pots, stones, soil, water. plants or seeds

GRAMMAR AND VOCABULARY:

Adverbs of manner: *gently, firmly, carefully, slowly*

NOTES:

1. To reduce the amount of material needed, you could do the procedure, talking about it as you do it, and then have the students retell what happened in the past tense.

2. After the plants have been planted, on succeeding days you could point to the plant and and say, "How did you do that?"

3. A similar procedure could be planting seeds.

2.9 Changing Batteries in a Flashlight *(Page 20)*

MATERIALS: Flashlights, batteries

GRAMMAR AND VOCABULARY:

1. Noun phrases: old batteries, two new batteries, positive ends

2. Phrasal verbs: *turn on, throw away*

3. Idiomatic *make sure*

NOTES:

1. Follow up with something else that has batteries — a toy, camera, clock.

2. Another variation: replace the bulb.

2.10 Greeting a Guest *(Page 21)*

MATERIALS: None

GRAMMAR AND VOCABULARY:

Deletion of subject and verb: *(It's) good to see you.*
(I've been) fine, thanks.

NOTES:

1. This ritual could be done with three people. The last line leads into another round of welcoming words.

2. After practicing the ritual, two students can serve as hosts and welcome the other students one at a time as if they were having a party.

2.11 Taking Leave *(Page 21)*

MATERIALS: None

GRAMMAR AND VOCABULARY:

1. Phrasal modal *have to*

2. Future modal *will*

3. Contractions in informal speech: *It's, I'm, I've, that's, you'll*

4. Idiomatic *I'm afraid so*

NOTES:

1. This ritual can follow 2.10 "Greeting a Guest."

2. After the students practice the ritual in pairs, you can have them do this as they leave the classroom. You act as the host as each student leaves.

Teaching Notes

Games and Exercises

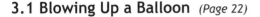

3.1 Blowing Up a Balloon *(Page 22)*

MATERIALS: Balloons

GRAMMAR AND VOCABULARY:

    1. *Until* clause

    2. Contractions: *it's, doesn't*

NOTES:
    Have the students use *after* and *will* before doing steps 2 through 6.
    "After I stretch the balloon, I will put the open end to my lips," etc.

3.2 Hopping on One Leg *(Page 22)*

MATERIALS: None

GRAMMAR AND VOCABULARY: Imperatives for actions, body parts

NOTES:
    1. Add transition words: *first, next, now*

    2. Have the students create similar procedures. They can try to use words such as *step, walk, skip, jump, leap.*

3.3 Touching Your Toes *(Page 23)*

MATERIALS: None

GRAMMAR AND VOCABULARY:

    Adverbials: *up over your head, from the waist*, etc.

NOTES:
    1. You may want to precede this activity with a review of the terms for the body.

    2. You could have students demonstrate and talk about other exercises such as push ups, sit ups.

3.4 Doing Jumping Jacks *(Page 23)*

MATERIALS: None

GRAMMAR AND VOCABULARY:

Adverbials: *to your sides, out to the side, up over your head*, etc.

NOTES:

1. After practicing in pairs or small groups, one student can lead the class in jumping jacks, giving commands: *swing, bring, again, again.*

2. Combine this activity with the previous two, mixing up the commands: *hop, jump, touch, jump*, etc.

3.5 Playing Jacks *(Page 24)*

MATERIALS: Jacks, a small rubber ball

GRAMMAR AND VOCABULARY:

1. Time clauses: *before, until*

2. Directional phrases: *onto the floor, into the air*

3. *Let* followed by bare infinitive(*bounce*)

NOTES:

1. You may have to demonstrate the game first.

2. Use the illustration as cues, with or instead of the sentences.

3. Have one student describe the action as if it is an athletic contest: "She's holding the ball. She's getting ready to toss the ball. She tossed it. She did it! She picked up a jack."

4. Hold a contest to see who can pick up the most without letting the ball hit the floor twice.

Teaching Notes

3.6 Playing Dice *(Page 25)*

MATERIALS: Dice

GRAMMAR AND VOCABULARY:

1. Locative prepositional phrase: *on top of*

2. Noun phrases: *the same number, the next player, the same thing, all the numbers*

3. *Until* clause

NOTES:

1. Each student will need a score sheet.

2. Create another game with dice.

3. Have a student create a procedure for dominoes or a simple card game such as "Slap Jack."

3.7 Setting Up a Chessboard *(Page 26)*

MATERIALS: Chess board and pieces

GRAMMAR AND VOCABULARY:

Locative prepositional phrases: *next to, beside, between,* etc.

NOTES:

1. It may be necessary to identify the pieces before doing the procedure.

2. Note the synonyms for "put."

3. Have a student demonstrate and describe the moves the pieces make.

4. Do a similar procedure for checkers or Chinese checkers.

3.8 Would You Please *(Page 27)*

MATERIALS: None

GRAMMAR AND VOCABULARY:

Present participle after *would you mind*

NOTES:

1. This is a variation of "Simon Says." You will need to explain the procedure before doing it. The students only perform the action if you say "Would you mind," or "Would you please."

2. First use the command verbs in the procedure: *touch, jump, turn.* Then introduce a few others: *bend, point, open, close.*

3. After you have led the class a few times, have students take turns leading.

3.9 Negotiating an Invitation *(Page 27)*

MATERIALS: None

GRAMMAR AND VOCABULARY:

1. Inclusive imperative *let's*

2. Phrasal modal *would rather*

NOTES:

1. Give the students the option to vary the ritual, as long as it is grammatical and colloquial. The fourth line, for example, has two options.

2. Introduce *let's not.*

3. After pairs have practiced, have them stage their dialogues for the rest of the class.

4. You can have pairs create invitations to other activities: watching a TV program, choosing a movie, deciding on dinner.

Teaching Notes Do As I Say

Games and Exercises

4.1 Eating a Banana *(Page 28)*

MATERIALS: Bananas, wastebaskets

GRAMMAR AND VOCABULARY:

1. Collocation of *take* and *a bite*

2. Completive phrasal verb: *chew up*

3. *Throw* vs. *throw away*

4. Present participle after *continue*

NOTES:

1. Similar procedures can be done with other fruits and vegetables.

2. Substitute *keep on* (continuative phrasal) for *continue*.

3. Have the students "walk through" the procedure before they actually start to eat the banana. When it is consumed, practice "What did you do?"

4.2 Making a Cup of Tea *(Page 28)*

MATERIALS: cups, tea bags, sugar, cream/milk, stirrers

GRAMMAR AND VOCABULARY:

1. Non-count nouns: *tea, water, milk, sugar*. Use of *some* as indefinite article

2. *A tea bag* vs. *tea*

3. *If* clauses

4. *Let* followed by a bare infinitive (*steep*)

NOTES:

1. If there is only one source of heat, have the students simulate making the tea in pairs. In the meantime, you boil several cups of water. Then, one-by-one, they actually make their cups of tea.

2. You could bring in several kinds of tea, and have the pairs negotiate which kind they prefer (see 3.9).

4.3 Making Instant Pudding *(Page 29)*

MATERIALS: A package of instant pudding, milk, bowl, spoons

GRAMMAR AND VOCABULARY:

1. Imperatives linked by *and*: *Open and pour*

2. Referential *it* as object. *Pour it,* etc.

NOTES:

1. Use the illustration with or instead of the sentences.

2. Have the students combine sentences 3 and 4 with *and* (*add and stir*) and sentences 5 and 6 (*pour and allow*).

3. If having enough material is a problem, do a demo without actually making the pudding. Then have the students practice the procedure in pairs, and finally, have them give you directions as you make the pudding.

4.4 Making a Peanut Butter and Jelly Sandwich *(Page 30)*

MATERIALS: Knife, bread, peanut butter, jelly

GRAMMAR AND VOCABULARY:

1. Non-count nouns (*bread, peanut butter, jelly*)

2. Associative preposition: *slice of bread*

NOTES:

1. Use the illustration with or instead of the sentences.

2. Begin the procedure by making a sandwich "for yourself," talking about it as you do it. Then have pairs practice the procedure without the materials, and finally have them give you instructions that you will follow precisely, even if the instruction is not clear. For example, if they say "Take the bread out of the package," you take it <u>all</u> out, not just two slices.

4.5 Making Spaghetti *(Page 31)*

MATERIALS: Spaghetti, water, pot, colander, burner or hot plate

GRAMMAR AND VOCABULARY:

1. *Let* followed by bare infinitive.

2. Uses of *for: wait for, boil for, for softness*

3. Meaning of *say (the directions say)*

4. *If* clause.

NOTES:

1. Demonstrate the steps of the procedure first. Give commands to yourself: "Read the directions." Then "I'm reading the directions." And then ask "What did I do?" After the students have practiced in pairs, have one pair volunteer to perform the procedure as others give commands and make comments.

2. This can be followed by creating a procedure for making a complete spaghetti dinner with sauce, cheese, garlic bread, salad, etc.

3. Go on to "Eating Spaghetti," 4.6.

4.6 Eating Spaghetti *(Page 31)*

MATERIALS: Plates, utensils, spaghetti, sauce, grated cheese

GRAMMAR AND VOCABULARY:

1. Non-count nouns: *spaghetti, sauce, cheese*

2. *Let* followed by bare infinitive

NOTES:

1. Do this after you have made spaghetti (4.5).

2. Put just the verbs on the board: *use, put, sprinkle, let.* etc. Go through the sentences a few times with the students listening, and then have pairs work together to re-create the seven sentences. They write them down, and then you give them the handout. Finally, have a spaghetti dinner if there's enough to go around.

4.7 Making a Cup of Instant Coffee *(Page 32)*

MATERIALS: Instant coffee, cups, spoons, milk, sugar, water, hot plate

GRAMMAR AND VOCABULARY:

1. Non-count nouns: *water, coffee, sugar, milk*

2. *If* clause

NOTES:

1. It may be best to demonstrate the procedure as the class watches and listens. Then have them pair up and try to reconstruct the sequence. Then hand out the sentences. And finally, have them tell you how to do it. If there's enough water, make coffee for everyone as they tell you how to do it.

2. A pair tells you how to make coffee. One student gives the commands; you follow, and the other student tells the class, "The teacher has just . . '

4.8 Making Coffee with a Coffeemaker *(Page 32)*

MATERIALS: Drip coffeemaker, ground coffee, scoop, filters, water

GRAMMAR AND VOCABULARY:

1. *Of* as genitive (*door of, inside of, top of*) and partitive (*scoops of, cups of*)

2. Other prepositions following verbs: *put around, put into, fill with, fill to, pour in.* And phrasal verbs: *take out, turn on*

NOTES:

1. Have one student come to the front and follow your directions as you make a small amount of coffee. Then have pairs practice the sequence, and finally, have one pair make the coffee, while the rest of the class practices "What is he going to do? What is he doing?" etc.

2. When the coffee is ready, follow up with a variation of the previous procedure: filling a cup, adding milk, sugar, and stirring.

4.9 Ordering a Cup of Coffee *(Page 33)*

MATERIALS: None required, although a coffee set up as prop could be useful

GRAMMAR AND VOCABULARY:

Polite expressions: *May I, I'd like, please*

NOTES:

1. After practicing this ritual, you play the role of server, and each student stands in line and orders a coffee.

2. You could also make it more complicated by offering different varieties: French roast, hazelnut, etc.

3. After doing this as a ritual, have the students write it up as a procedure: "First, you tell the server if you want regular or decaf. Then you say if you want sugar." etc.

4. Have the students do this at a coffee shop as homework.

4.10 Making Popcorn *(Page 33)*

MATERIALS: Popcorn popper, popcorn, measuring cup, butter, salt, bowls

GRAMMAR AND VOCABULARY:

1. *While* and *when* clauses

2. Prepositions: *into, over, on*

3. Non-count nouns: *popcorn, butter, salt* with *the* or *some*

NOTES:

1. Put the verbs on the board and tell the students what they "are going to do." In pairs they practice saying what they "are going to do." Then they have to tell you perfectly what you are going to do. You make the popcorn. Everybody has some popcorn and talks about how you made it.

2. Bring in needle and thread and make a "popcorn chain." See 2.5 "Threading a Needle."

4.11 Ordering a Pizza for Delivery *(Page 34)*

MATERIALS: (optional) An order form from a local pizza parlor

GRAMMAR AND VOCABULARY:

1. Relative clause: *that you want*

2. Embedded WH clause: *How much it will be*

NOTES:

1. The students practice the procedure in pairs. Then when they are ready, they tell you "how to do it."

2. After doing this as a procedure, do it as a dialogue, with one person "on the phone" ordering, and the other at the pizza parlor, taking the order.

3. Have a pizza party and call out for two or three different small pizzas.

4.12 Using a Fast Food Drive-Through *(Page 34)*

MATERIALS: ((optional) A menu from a drive-through

GRAMMAR AND VOCABULARY:

Collocated verb and preposition: *wait for, pay for*

NOTES:

1. This could also be done as a ritual dialogue.

2. Take photos (get permission) of different drive-up signs (burger, chicken, tacos) photocopy and and give them to the students for practicing the ritual. When they are ready, they tell each other what they "ordered, " and how much it cost.

4.13 Eating in a Restaurant *(Page 35)*

MATERIALS: (optional) Table and chairs, table setting, menu, order book

GRAMMAR AND VOCABULARY:

1. Modal *will*, contracted, meaning "willingness"

2. Phrasal modal *would like to*

NOTES:

1. This would be a little more natural if done as threes — one server, two customers. But it can easily be done by pairs, just change "Here are your drinks." to "Here is your drink."

2. Menus would be very helpful

4.14 Shopping in a Supermarket *(Page 35)*

MATERIALS: (optional) a Shopping list

GRAMMAR AND VOCABULARY:

1. Relative clause with optional *that* : *the items (that) you need*

2. *Check, check-out* and *check off*

NOTES:

1. To provide some realia, you could prepare a shopping list, or have the students make one, or bring in supermarket flyers.

2. Follow up with a check-out ritual between the cashier and the shopper. "Hello — any coupons? — paper or plastic? — That'll be $ — Have a good day."

3. You could have them pay for their "purchases" with a check (using photocopies of the check on page 43).

Do As I Say

Communication

5.1 Mailing a Letter *(Page 36)*

MATERIALS: Paper, envelopes, pens, stamps

GRAMMAR AND VOCABULARY:

1. Locative phrases: *in the corner, on the front*

2. Infinitive as adverb: "Fold the letter <u>to fit</u> the envelope."

NOTES:

1. Have the students talk through the procedure before finally doing it.

2. Used stamps and a glue stick will save money.

3. When finished, they can bring the letter to the post office (you) for checking.

5.2 Buying Stamps *(Page 36)*

MATERIALS: Stamps, receipt slips

GRAMMAR AND VOCABULARY:

Polite expressions

NOTES:

1. This ritual can follow up on the previous procedure.
2. Used stamps will save money.
3. After pairs have practiced, they can come to you one at a time to "buy stamps."
4. You could have them ask for a special commemorative stamp.

Teaching Notes Do As I Say

5.3 Using a Pay Telephone *(Page 37)*

MATERIALS: (optional) A play phone, coins or a drawing of a pay phone

GRAMMAR AND VOCABULARY:

    1. Relative clause: *the number <u>that</u> you are calling*
    2. *Until* clause

NOTES:

    1. Use the illustration with or without the sentences.
    2. Try variations such as a long distance or collect call.
    3. Follow up with the next sequence: "Leaving a Message."

5.4 Leaving a Message *(Page 38)*

MATERIALS: (optional) A play phone, additional copies
                of the sample recorded message

GRAMMAR AND VOCABULARY:

    1. Time clauses with *after* and *when*

    2. Gerunds: *speaking, recording*

NOTES:

    1. Provide the sample recorded message on the next page.

    2. After pairs practice the sequence, they can do the message
       as a monologue.

5.5 Using a Phone Card *(Page 39)*

MATERIALS: A play phone, additional copies of the sample phone card

GRAMMAR AND VOCABULARY:

    1. Reduced relative clause: *time (that is) remaining on your card*

    2. Relative clauses: *the number you want to call, the person who answers*

NOTES:

    1. Make copies of the sample phone card.

    2. At step #6, combine this procedure with the previous
       sequence, "Leaving a Message."

5.6 Wiring Money *(Page 40)*

MATERIALS: Copies of the money order form on the next page

GRAMMAR AND VOCABULARY:

    1. Reduced relative clause: *the person (who is) at the desk*

    2. Complement with *that*: <u>*that*</u> *you want . . .*

    3. Infinitive as complement clause: *you want <u>to wire</u> some money.*

NOTES:

    1. Photocopy the form. Before doing the sequence, go over the form with the class.

    2. After pairs have practiced the procedure, they can fill out the form. Then they bring it to you to hand it in and "pay" for it.

5.7 Receiving an Email *(Page 41)*

MATERIALS: (optional) A computer

GRAMMAR AND VOCABULARY:

    1. Subordinate *if* clause: *If you want to answer*

    2. Complement with *if*: decide *if you want . . .*

NOTES:

    1. If the students are not familiar with email, you may have to give them an introductory lesson on it.

    2. This procedure may need to be revised for some email systems.

    3. If possible, demonstrate this operation to the class with a computer. Then have them practice the operation verbally. If computers are available, they can exchange emails with each other.

5.8 Using a FAX machine *(Page 41)*

MATERIALS: A FAX machine, paper with message

GRAMMAR AND VOCABULARY:

    1. Passive infinitive: *to be faxed*

    2. Infinitive phrase of purpose: *to be sure*

    3. Passive voice: *was received*

NOTES:

    1. First, demonstrate the use of a FAX machine, if possible.

    2. As a variation, have the students use the impersonal "you,"as if they were teaching someone how to use the machine. "First, <u>you</u> look over the message, then <u>you</u> feed the paper, etc."

5.9 Making a Plane Reservation on the Internet *(Page 42)*

MATERIALS: A Computer

GRAMMAR AND VOCABULARY: Imperatives for computer actions, travel terms

NOTES:

    1. Web sites are not all alike. You may have to modify the procedure to fit a particular web.

    2. If possible, demonstrate the procedure with a computer.

    3. Have the students create an itinerary, and then when they have practiced the procedure, tell what they did, where they plan to go, and when.

5.10 Searching the Internet *(Page 42)*

MATERIALS: A computer

GRAMMAR AND VOCABULARY:

    1. Verb-preposition collocations: *click on, type in*

    2. Phrasal verbs: *turn on, check out*

NOTES:

    1. If possible, demonstrate a search on the web.

    2. After practicing the sentences, if a computer is available, have one or more pairs do a search.

Around Town

6.1 Writing a Check *(Page 43)*

MATERIALS: Check and register illustration

GRAMMAR AND VOCABULARY:

1. 's possessive: *today's* date, *payee's* name

2. Prepositions: *in* as manner adverbial, *on* as locative, *of* as associative

NOTES:

1. Make copies of the check and register. You may want each pair to write more than one check.

2. Have the students write the instructions using *after* and *before*.

3. Have the students ask each other "where" questions: "Where did you write the date?" etc.

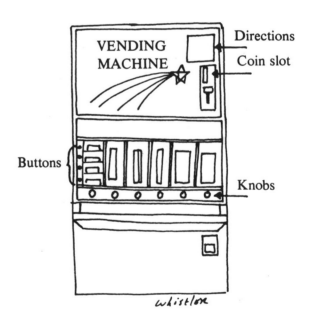

6.2 Using a Vending Machine *(Page 44)*

MATERIALS: The illustration

GRAMMAR AND VOCABULARY:

1. Compound nouns: *vending machine, money slot*

2. Compound sentence with *or*

NOTES:

If there is a vending machine nearby, make purchases after practicing the operation. The students should describe what they're going to do and what they did.

6.3 Filling in a Form *(Page 45, 46)*

MATERIALS: Copies of the application on page 46

GRAMMAR AND VOCABULARY:

Possessive with time: *today's date*

NOTES:

1. First, be sure the students understand the form.

2. Have the students practice the procedure before filling in the form.

3. Bring in other forms for additional practice.

4. Discuss the importance of privacy and the danger of giving out personal information — especially social security numbers.

6.4 Using an ATM Card *(Page 45)*

MATERIALS: None

GRAMMAR AND VOCABULARY:

1. Relative clause: *the amount you want to withdraw*

2. Infinitive as complement: *want to withdraw*

NOTES:

1. This operation could be done as an instruction using the impersonal "you:" "How do you use an ATM? First, you read the directions," etc.

2. Another variation could be to have students work on what they "are going to do" when they go to an ATM.

6.5 Renting a DVD *(Page 47)*

MATERIALS: None

GRAMMAR AND VOCABULARY: Situation specific vocabulary

NOTES:

1. The same procedure can apply to renting a video cassette or video game.

2. The procedure could be followed up with a typical check-out dialogue.

3. Methods of payment vary and can be added to the procedure.

4. This could be followed with discussion on "My favorite films."

6.6 Finding an Apartment *(Page 47)*

MATERIALS: (OPTIONAL) Classified ad section of a newspaper

GRAMMAR AND VOCABULARY:

1. *It* as complementizer: *Ask if it's available*

2. Conditional if: *If it sounds good*

3. Linking verb *sound*, followed by adjective

NOTES:

1. You could begin with some work on reading classified ads for apartments and understnding the abbreviations and terminology.

2. After doing the procedure, the students can do telephone dialogues for steps 6,7, and 8.

6.7 Using a Laundromat *(Page 48)*

MATERIALS: None

GRAMMAR AND VOCABULARY:

1. When clause: *When the machine is finished*

2. Past participle as adjective: *finished*

NOTES:

After the pairs have finished the practice, you can have them respond to: "What are you going to do when you go to a laundromat?"

6.8 Using a Self-Service Gas Pump *(Page 48)*

MATERIALS: None

GRAMMAR AND VOCABULARY:

1. Relative clause: *the grade of gas <u>that you want</u>*

2. Past participle as adjective: *finished*

NOTES:

1. Introduce the operation as a pantomime, and ask the students to figure out what you are doing.

2. Do a variation involving full-service.

Teaching Notes

6.9 Starting a Car *(Page 49)*

MATERIALS: None

GRAMMAR AND VOCABULARY:

1. Imperative *Be.* with adjective: *sure*

2. Compound sentences: *Open the door and get in. Turn the key and step on the gas. Shift into drive and step on the gas.*

NOTES:

1. You may need to precede this with a vocabulary review of the parts of a car.

2. Introduce the operation as a pantomime, and ask the students to figure out what you are doing.

3. Do a variation with a stick shift.

6.10 Checking in at the Airport *(Page 49)*

MATERIALS: (Optional) tickets, ID cards

GRAMMAR AND VOCABULARY:

When clause. *When it's your turn*

NOTES:

1. Have the students prepare imaginary tickets.

2. Create a dialogue for the check-in procedure.

3. After they have finished practicing, have them line up and go one-by-one through a dialogue with you as the airline person.

Other books from Pro Lingua

Index Card Games for ESL. 7 games using index cards to learn vocabulary, practice grammar structures, and build confidence and competence in conversation. For each game there are photocopyable samples that are easy, moderate, and difficult.

More Index Card Games for English. 9 more games using index cards appropriate for students at different proficiency levels. These games stress speaking and listening skills. As in Index Card Games for ESL, though in a smaller format, all the sample material is photocopyable.

Match It! Another photocopyable collection of index card games. The game "Match It!" is similar to "Concentration." The materials range in difficulty from basic/easy to advanced/difficult.

Pronunciation Card Games. A photocopyable collection of index card games working on minimal pairs, syllabification, stress, and intonation.

The Great Big BINGO Book. A photocopyable collection of bingo games, providing practice with grammar, vocabulary, writing, pronunciation, and cultural information.

Shenanigames. 49 games practicing specific grammar points of graded difficulty. They are appropriate for students from middle school to adult.

The ESL Miscellany. A single-volume teacher resource book with dozens of lists of grammatical information, vocabulary topics, cultural information, miscellaneous material (punctuation rules, spelling rules, abbreviations, maps, gestures, etc.). A great resource for developing games and other lesson materials.

Lexicarry. Hundreds of uncaptioned pictures which get students talking about language, learning vocabulary, and discussing what language is appropriate in the pictured situations. Includes functions, sequences, operations, topics, and proverbs. Ideal for pair and small group work. A word list in the back allows for self-study. Wordlists in other languages and a teacher's guide are free at www.Lexicarry.com. Over 4500 words.

English Interplay: Surviving. A first text for beginning adolescents and adults. Students work in pairs, triads, and small groups, learning basic grammar, spelling, pronunciation, numbers, and a 700-word vocabulary that is necessary for survival in an English-speaking world.

Rhymes and Rhythms. 32 original poems/chants for practicing basic grammar and pronunciation and learning vocabulary. The rhymes progress from short and easy to longer and more challenging. This is a photocopyable text with an optional CD recording of all the rhymes read once deliberately and then read again at natural speed.

Pro Lingua Associates • 800-366-4775
www.ProLinguaAssociates.com